EARTH'S HISTORY

Please visit our web site at: www.garethstevens.com
For a free color catalog describing Gareth Stevens Publishing's list of high-quality books and multimedia programs, call 1-800-542-2595 (USA) or 1-800-387-3178 (Canada). Gareth Stevens Publishing's fax: (414) 332-3567.

Library of Congress Cataloging-in-Publication Data available upon request from publisher. Fax (414) 336-0157 for the attention of the Publishing Records Department.

ISBN 0-8368-3379-1

This edition first published in 2004 by
Gareth Stevens Publishing
A World Almanac Education Group Company
330 West Olive Street, Suite 100
Milwaukee, WI 53212 USA

Further resources for students and educators available at
www.discoveryschool.com

Designed by Bill SMITH STUDIO
Creative Director: Ron Leighton
Designers: Sonia Gauba, Nick Stone, Joe Bartos, Dmitri Kushnirsky, Bill Wilson, Darren, D'Agostino
Photo Editors: Jennifer Friel, Scott Haag
Art Buyers: Paula Radding, Marianne Tozzo

Gareth Stevens Editor: Betsy Rasmussen
Gareth Stevens Art Director: Tammy Gruenewald
Technical Advisor: Sara Bruening

Printed in the United States of America

1 2 3 4 5 6 7 8 9 08 07 06 05 04

Writers: Jackie Ball, Michael Burgan, Margaret Carruthers, Diane Webber

Editor: Lelia Mander

Photographs: Cover, geological strata, © Kerrick James/Tony Stone Images; p. 2, geological strata, © Kerrick James/Tony Stone Images; p. 3, world motif, MapArt; p. 10, Dr. Kendrick Taylor, team drilling for ice sample (both), © Gregg Lamorey; pp. 14-15, San Francisco earthquake of 1906 (both), Corbis/Bettmann; p. 16, Alfred Wegener, courtesy University of California, Berkeley; p. 18, Mt. St. Helens before and after eruption, PhotoDisc; p. 22, geological strata, © Kerrick James/Tony Stone Images; p. 24, fossil, ferns, geologist (all),

PhotoDisc; p. 25, underwater volcanic gases, © Fred McConnaughey /Photo Researchers, Inc.; p. 25, Cindy Lee Van Dover, courtesy Tom Kleindinst; p. 28, Meteor Crater, PhotoDisc; p. 29, Half Dome, Bryce Canyon, PhotoDisc; p. 30, piece of bread, PhotoDisc; all other photographs by Corel.

Illustrations: pp. 8-9, globes through the ages, Christopher Burke; pp. 20-21, glacier bobsled, Lee MacLeod.

Acknowledgments: pp. 14-15, excerpts from THREE FEARFUL DAYS by Malcolm E. Barker (ed.). © 1998 Londonborn Publications. Reprinted with permission.

CONTENTS

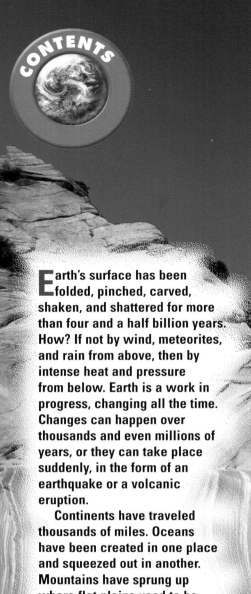

Earth's surface has been folded, pinched, carved, shaken, and shattered for more than four and a half billion years. How? If not by wind, meteorites, and rain from above, then by intense heat and pressure from below. Earth is a work in progress, changing all the time. Changes can happen over thousands and even millions of years, or they can take place suddenly, in the form of an earthquake or a volcanic eruption.

Continents have traveled thousands of miles. Oceans have been created in one place and squeezed out in another. Mountains have sprung up where flat plains used to be. Huge sheets of ice have carved out valleys and flattened hilltops before melting into the sea. We know this incredible story because it has been written on the rocky face of Earth itself.

Discovery Channel will take you through EARTH'S HISTORY, from its fiery beginnings to present day. Check out the mountains and canyons in Earth's crust and peer below the surface to dig up the real dirt about this planet with a past.

EARTH'S HISTORY

How did life get here? See page 25.

Final Project

History of Earth

Northern Arizona, Today

You're standing on the Kaibab Plateau in northern Arizona. The landscape appears to be a flat and endless expanse of rocky soil, pinyon bushes, and juniper trees. Now walk south 1 mile (1.6 kilometers) or so—the ground drops off into a gorge 1 mile (1.6 km) deep called the Grand Canyon. What you thought was the constant, unchanging Earth has really gone through dramatic change, as you can see in the rock.

And yet, only four million years ago, there was no Grand Canyon, just the beginnings of a river we now call the Colorado. The river began to erode the land, eventually carving the Grand Canyon out of the flat Arizona landscape.

The walls of the Grand Canyon tell a story that's five hundred times as old as the canyon itself. Over billions of years, Earth's surface has been built up, layer after layer. But nothing stays the same: These layers have been worn away by the forces of weather and erosion. See for yourself if you don't believe it.

IT'S SEDIMENTARY

Ever realize how many different colors there are in the Grand Canyon? Each layer represents a chapter in Earth's history, beginning two billion years ago. The pieces were added, layer by layer, over time.

Sediments are deposits of mud, stones, and other material collected at the bottom of lakes, rivers, and oceans. Over time, more layers are added. The combined weight eventually hardens these deposits into rock. Other changes take place, too—a lake may dry up, for example, or a volcano could release a flow of lava, adding yet another layer to the pile. And before you know it, there's another ocean covering the land and adding more sediments. These layers hold clues about Earth's atmosphere, its earliest life-forms, and all the changes the planet has seen over the years.

Utah

● GRAND CANYON

Arizona

New Mexico

Mexico

ERODE AWAY

It would be a lot harder for geologists to study these layers if they were all buried deep under the ground. But thanks to the unstoppable persistence of running water, we can see a fascinating cross section of our planet's story. Over the four million years of the Grand Canyon's history, water has cut into the ground and carried away pieces of it, bit by bit.

Running water isn't the only force behind erosion—weather gets into the act, too. As water strips away layers of rock, they are exposed to wind and rain. These forces gradually cut away at the banks, sculpting the land into the amazing shapes we see today.

Some say the Grand Canyon has never looked as magnificent as it does now. We'll never know for sure. But we do know one thing: No matter how deep, broad, and awesome the Grand Canyon is today, like everything else on Earth, it, too, will be worn away over time.

Growing Pains

Q: You're Earth, all green land and blue water and layers of red rock with just the right accents of wispy white clouds and snow-covered peaks. How do you stay so—well, pretty?

A: It hasn't been easy. And I didn't always look this way. Beauty like this took billions of years—four and a half billion to be exact—and a lot of pain.

Q: Pain?

A: You wouldn't believe how I've suffered. I've been pummeled and pounded, blasted and bombarded, fried, flooded, and frozen over.

Q: Gee, that's terrible. How did it begin?

A: First, there was a big, noisy explosion of hot minerals and gases, and the Sun and planets formed. You wouldn't have recognized me. I was nothing but a big fireball, covered with melted rock. Then I got pounded with hunks of metal and rock from outer space that made big gouges, holes, and craters all over me.

Q: Ouch!

A: Yeah, but things were only beginning. Gravity pulled the heaviest stuff, hot iron, down into my center. It's still there, only it's solid now. And on top, a crust started to form.

Q: You mean like a bread crust?

A: No, more like a skin. As it cooled, it cracked. And the cracks are still there in my crust, but now you've given them a name: the edges of tectonic plates. These cracks turned out to be very helpful.

saturated. One hundred percent humidity. In other words . . .

Q: Millions of years of bad hair days?

A: No, rain! Loads of it. Tons and tons of it. Pouring down and cooling things off. But not too much. It was still pretty warm on Earth.

Q: I'll bet. But if everything was underwater, where did the continents come from?

A: They came from under the ocean. Magma under my crust seeped and squeezed its way up to form islands. More and more islands formed—so many that they all crowded together and formed one super-big continent.

Q: Only one continent? I thought there were seven.

A: Back then there was just one great big one. Anyway, before long—about three and a half billion years ago—I had water AND oxygen. The oxygen was made by tiny creatures who used sunlight to make energy. Without them, all the life at that time couldn't have flourished the way it did. Plants. Animals. Dinosaurs. Little mammals. Then one day, something big hit me. Could have been a meteor.

Q: That sounds like trouble.

A: The worst kind of trouble: A mass extinction wiped out most

Q: How?

A: Because volcanic eruptions bubbled through them. Lava flowed and built new land. Gases came belching out, forming the atmosphere. Of course you couldn't breathe it then. It was like a big, wet, smelly blanket wrapped around me. But it paved the way.

Q: Paved the way for what?

A: Water. The wet stuff. That damp smelly gas made things so moist that it didn't take much— maybe a bunch of ice comets hit me or something—to make the atmosphere completely

of the large animals on Earth. Acid rain dimmed the Sun. It got cold, and then icy, and . . . well, that's history.

Q: I bet you're glad that violent part of your history is over.

A: Over? It's never over. Earth is in constant change. Every day I'm peppered with space rocks. If that's not enough, I'm being scoured and sculpted and cut by the wind. And water's the strongest force. It can cut through solid rock—given enough time.

Q: So how come you're not as flat as a pancake, with all these forces grinding at you?

A: Because rocks are constantly being pushed up to the surface by my constant movement and shifting. Think of it as kind of a facelift. Anyway, that's the story of my life: push and pull, wear and tear. It's my story, and I'm sticking to it. Actually, I'm stuck WITH it.

Q: Any idea what's ahead for Earth?

A: Oh, another catastrophe. Collision. Ice Age. Something.

Q: Yikes! When do you think it's going to happen?

A: Could be any time, or could be in a few million years. Hard to tell. But meanwhile, where can I get a really big, really heavy-duty hard hat?

Activity

MAKE YOUR OWN Trace the continents as shown on the map on pages 12–13, and cut them out. Blow up a balloon to a diameter of about five inches. Work with a friend to fit the continents on the balloon to show how Earth looked before the land "drifted" into the seven continents.

Globes Through the Ages

Precambrian:
4,600 mya to 544 mya

4,600 Million Years Ago	4,000 MYA	3,500 MYA	3000 MYA	2,500 MYA

No Life on Earth

4.5 Billion Years Ago

In the beginning, Earth's temperature is so hot that the entire surface is a sea of molten rock, or magma, hundreds of miles (km) deep. Slowly, as the surface cools, heavier metals (such as iron and nickel) settle to the core, and on the surface, a crust begins to form. But there is still a lot of heat trapped inside, producing volcanoes, and the surface is still too hot for water to exist in any state except as water vapor. If there is an atmosphere, it is probably mainly carbon dioxide, with nitrogen and water vapor, all belched out of volcanoes. Comets and meteorites are continually bombarding the surface, but Earth doesn't yet have a moon, and there is no life, as we know it.

3.5 Billion Years Ago

As the planet cools, water vapor condenses and forms the oceans. Water spewed by volcanoes and brought in from outer space by comets covers much of Earth. The Moon is in Earth's orbit, closer than it is now. Life is beginning to take hold in the ocean: Colonies of single-celled bacteria bask in sunlight near the ocean surface. As they convert sunlight into food, these organisms give off oxygen. Meanwhile on land, the continents are growing. New landforms as volcanoes erupt. Small land masses collide with each other to form larger ones. Without enough oxygen in the atmosphere, these areas are completely bare of vegetation.

500 Million Years Ago

Life is thriving and evolving in the oceans. Trilobites swim over the seafloor. Reefs of coral are growing in the warm, shallow seas at the edges of the supercontinents Gondwana and Laurentia. And the dry land, which has been bare rock, completely without life, is perhaps slowly turning green with small forms of algae. As a result, oxygen is quickly building up in the atmosphere. Soon the land and air will be ready to support such life-forms as plants, insects, and reptiles.

Earth has been around a long time. Along with the Sun and the other planets in our Solar System, it was formed about 4.6 billion years ago. Although this doesn't look like a big number in writing, keep in mind that *one* billion actually equals a *thousand* million. That's a lot of years! And for a long time, Earth was no great place to live. In the beginning, the planet was so hot that the entire surface was a sea of liquid rock. As it cooled, crust began to form. Pieces of the thin crust began to float on the molten rock; volcanoes erupted; and continents began to grow. Water accumulated on the surface, and the oceans grew larger. At first, there was very little oxygen, although the air was full of gases, thanks to the volcanoes. But as bacteria and plants evolved and grew, they breathed oxygen into the water and air.

Paleozoic: 544 mya to 245 mya

Mesozoic: 245 mya to 65 mya

Cenozoic: 65 mya to present day

2000 MYA   1,500 MYA   1,000 MYA   500 MYA   Now

Life in Oceans Only   Life Starts on Land

50,000 Years Ago

Earth is in the middle of an ice age. The temperature averages 9°F (5°C) cooler than today. Because it is so cold, ice sheets spread out from the North and South poles, covering much of North America, northern Europe, and Siberia. More and more water is frozen into the ice sheets, causing the level of the oceans to be 200 feet (61 meters) lower than today. Also, there is more dry land: Great Britain is connected to the rest of Europe; a land bridge links Siberia to Alaska; and Australia and New Guinea are one land mass. Human beings live in Africa, southern Europe, and Asia.

Activity

MAKE IT COUNT Counting in billions of years makes it hard to grasp how old our planet really is. Here's a way to picture the length of time. Imagine the whole history of Earth is shortened to one year. January 1 is the date when Earth forms into the sphere we call a planet. Here are some other key dates during the year:

> **February 21**—First life appears
>
> **October 25**—Shellfish appear
>
> **November 20**—Fish appear
>
> **December 15**—Dinosaurs appear
>
> **December 25**—Dinosaurs become extinct
>
> **December 31, 11:00 P.M.**—Appearance of *Homo erectus*
>
> **December 31, 11:59:57 P.M.**—Christopher Columbus sails to America

Make a horizontal time line of this information. Divide it evenly into twelve months, and mark each of these dates on the time line. Comparing your time line with the geological scale, determine in which era each event occurred. You can also measure the distances between each of the dates to come up with proportions.

Here's the DRILL

Dr. Ken Taylor holding a wooden case containing an ice-core sample from Antarctica.

Siple Dome, Antarctica, 1999

From November through January, Dr. Kendrick Taylor and his colleagues get out of the lab—way out of the lab. Their work takes them thousands of miles away, to one of the most remote places on Earth.

Each year during the Southern Hemisphere's summer months (the same as our winter months), a handful of researchers from all over the world head for Antarctica. Their mission: to unlock the secrets of Earth's past, which have been stored for thousands of years in the Antarctic ice shelf.

Taylor calls ice from Earth's poles "the museum of climate," because it preserves information about the weather going back 100,000 years. To get this information, scientists drill into the ice and pull out long tubes, called ice cores. Usually, the cores are about 6 inches (15 centimeters) in diameter and are carefully divided into 2-meter (7-foot) lengths. "They look like logs made of ice," says Taylor, who is a lead scientist on the West Antarctic Ice Sheet coring project, known as WAISCORES.

ANCIENT SECRETS IN THE ICE

A trained eye can see layers in the ice cores, where snow stacked up year after year. Using very sophisticated techniques and equipment, such as mass spectrometers and ion chromatographs, scientists collect all sorts of data about the ancient atmosphere. Chemicals that were dissolved in the snow as it fell— called soluble materials—can be examined. And insoluble materials, such as dust particles caught in the spaces between snowflakes, can also be identified.

Among the facts frozen in time are: the temperature, the amount of snowfall, wind speed, air circulation, size of the nearest wetlands, and whether there were any large fires or volcanic eruptions. Evidence from the ice cores, for example, have confirmed the eruption of Mount Vesuvius in Italy, in 79 A.D.

The researchers and the other members of their team—cooks, mechanics, drill operators—fly first to New Zealand and then to McMurdo Station on the coast of Antarctica. They spend a week or two there checking their equipment and gear before going out to the drilling site. You can't afford to forget anything if you're planning to spend three months living at temperatures below -10°F! (-23°C) This is also everyone's last chance to use the phone or send out lengthy e-mails.

CAMPING OUT IN THE COLD
A C-130 airplane loaded with their equipment takes the team to the WAISCORES site at a location called Siple Dome. "It's a three-hour flight over nothing but ice—no towns, no buildings, no trees," says Taylor. When the plane arrives, it lands on skis instead of wheels.

At the camp, scientists and crew members each have their own unheated tent for sleeping. They eat meals together in a heated building, and they hop on snowmobiles to get to the drill site.

The scientists supervise the ice drilling, and then they carefully measure and catalog the core samples. Some experiments must be performed immediately because transporting the ice would change the results. Other tests can wait until the samples have been shipped in refrigerated cases back to labs in the United States.

HOW DID THE ICE AGE END?
Taylor and his team are drilling 980 meters (3,215 feet) into the ice sheet—all the way down to Antarctica's bedrock. The ice at the bottom is 100,000 years old. Their research will compare the last ice age to the warmer, wetter period we're in now. That global change in climate occurred about 11,700 years ago.

The Siple Dome cores have confirmed a startling fact discovered by earlier experiments in Greenland: The climate at the end of the ice age changed from cold to warm in only forty years. Although it took a few thousand years for all the ice to melt, the change that caused this great thaw happened much more quickly than scientists originally thought. It was more like a switch was flipped, rather than a gradual shift in temperature.

Now researchers are trying to find out where this dramatic change happened first—Greenland or Antarctica, Northern Hemisphere or Southern Hemisphere? Taylor hopes this will lead them to find out why. "If you heard a strange noise in your house, finding out whether it came from the kitchen or the bedroom would give you clues about what it was," Taylor says. The Siple Dome scientists are testing theories about whether ocean currents or atmospheric changes caused the sudden change.

This research has important implications for the environment today. The current high concentrations of greenhouse gases in the atmosphere could warm Earth significantly, and the ice-core evidence shows that this might happen much more quickly than previously thought possible.

"We can never know exactly what will happen until it actually occurs, but our role as scientists is to make the very best predictions we can about a course of action so that society as a whole can make informed decisions," says Taylor.

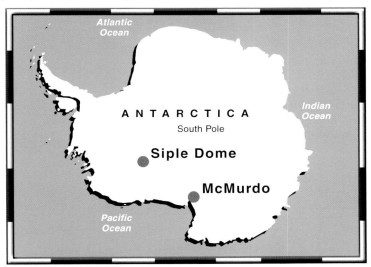

Atlantic Ocean

ANTARCTICA
South Pole

Indian Ocean

Siple Dome

McMurdo

Pacific Ocean

Activity

WEATHER REPORT Imagine you could examine an ice core of your town or region over the past 100 years. Do some research on the climate in your area over the past year, and create a scientific journal detailing the air quality, seasonal weather patterns, and other climatic events that took place. Compare that information to what Earth's climate was like 100 years ago in your area.

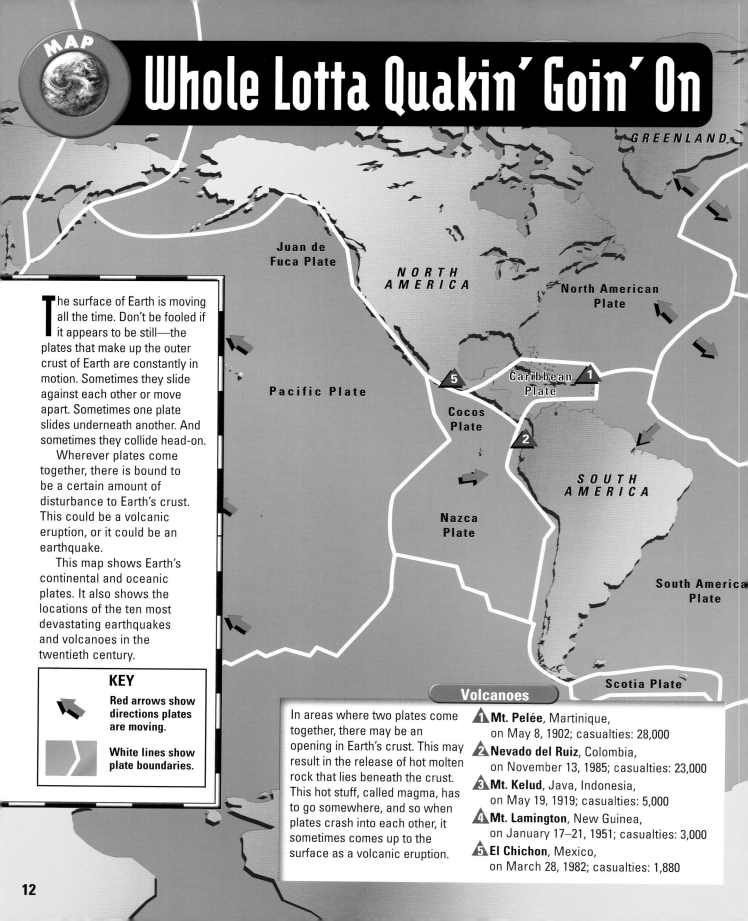

Whole Lotta Quakin' Goin' On

GREENLAND

Juan de
Fuca Plate

NORTH
AMERICA

North American
Plate

Pacific Plate

Caribbean
Plate

5

1

Cocos
Plate

2

SOUTH
AMERICA

Nazca
Plate

South America
Plate

Scotia Plate

The surface of Earth is moving all the time. Don't be fooled if it appears to be still—the plates that make up the outer crust of Earth are constantly in motion. Sometimes they slide against each other or move apart. Sometimes one plate slides underneath another. And sometimes they collide head-on.

Wherever plates come together, there is bound to be a certain amount of disturbance to Earth's crust. This could be a volcanic eruption, or it could be an earthquake.

This map shows Earth's continental and oceanic plates. It also shows the locations of the ten most devastating earthquakes and volcanoes in the twentieth century.

KEY

Red arrows show directions plates are moving.

White lines show plate boundaries.

Volcanoes

In areas where two plates come together, there may be an opening in Earth's crust. This may result in the release of hot molten rock that lies beneath the crust. This hot stuff, called magma, has to go somewhere, and so when plates crash into each other, it sometimes comes up to the surface as a volcanic eruption.

1 **Mt. Pelée**, Martinique, on May 8, 1902; casualties: 28,000

2 **Nevado del Ruiz**, Colombia, on November 13, 1985; casualties: 23,000

3 **Mt. Kelud**, Java, Indonesia, on May 19, 1919; casualties: 5,000

4 **Mt. Lamington**, New Guinea, on January 17–21, 1951; casualties: 3,000

5 **El Chichon**, Mexico, on March 28, 1982; casualties: 1,880

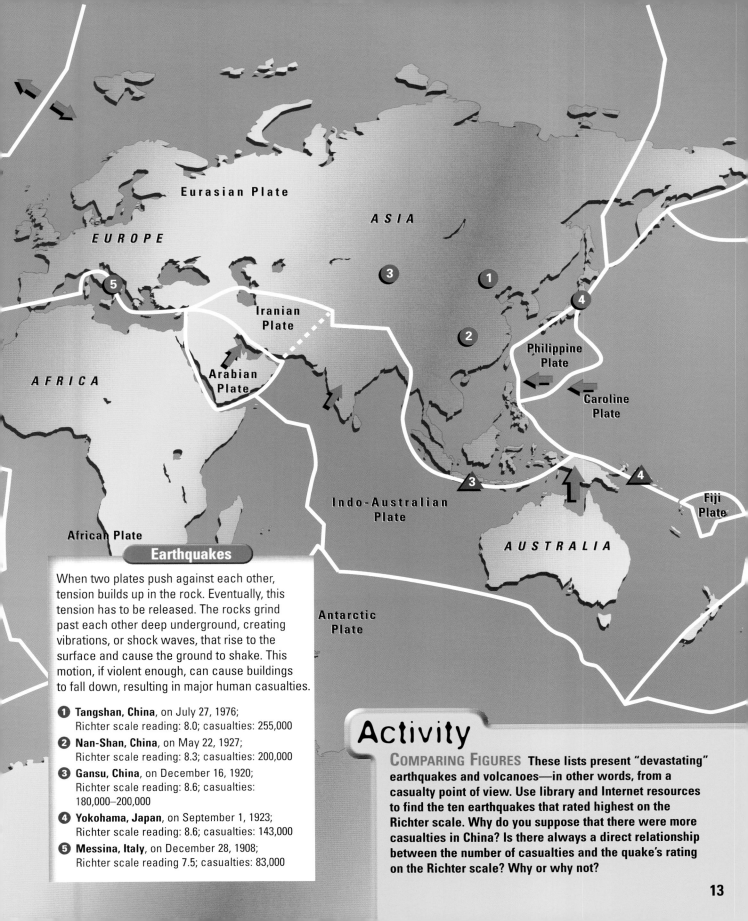

Eurasian Plate

ASIA

EUROPE

③

①

④

Iranian
Plate

Arabian
Plate

Philippine
Plate

AFRICA

Caroline
Plate

②

③

④

Indo-Australian
Plate

Fiji
Plate

African Plate

AUSTRALIA

Antarctic
Plate

Earthquakes

When two plates push against each other, tension builds up in the rock. Eventually, this tension has to be released. The rocks grind past each other deep underground, creating vibrations, or shock waves, that rise to the surface and cause the ground to shake. This motion, if violent enough, can cause buildings to fall down, resulting in major human casualties.

❶ **Tangshan, China**, on July 27, 1976;
Richter scale reading: 8.0; casualties: 255,000

❷ **Nan-Shan, China**, on May 22, 1927;
Richter scale reading: 8.3; casualties: 200,000

❸ **Gansu, China**, on December 16, 1920;
Richter scale reading: 8.6; casualties:
180,000–200,000

❹ **Yokohama, Japan**, on September 1, 1923;
Richter scale reading: 8.6; casualties: 143,000

❺ **Messina, Italy**, on December 28, 1908;
Richter scale reading 7.5; casualties: 83,000

Activity

COMPARING FIGURES **These lists present "devastating" earthquakes and volcanoes—in other words, from a casualty point of view. Use library and Internet resources to find the ten earthquakes that rated highest on the Richter scale. Why do you suppose that there were more casualties in China? Is there always a direct relationship between the number of casualties and the quake's rating on the Richter scale? Why or why not?**

13

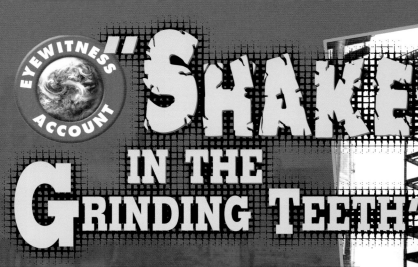

"SHAKEN IN THE GRINDING TEETH"

San Francisco, April 18, 1906, 5:12 A.M.

Most of the time, Earth is changing too slowly for people to notice. Mountains form over thousands of years; glaciers creep over the land inch by inch (cm) and then melt away. But there are moments when our timetable runs smack into Earth's, and people see violent, destructive changes firsthand.

Early one spring morning, the city of San Francisco was jolted awake by the worst earthquake in its history. The ground shook for almost one minute, toppling buildings, ripping open streets and avenues, and shattering windows for miles (km) around. And the worst was yet to come: the quake tore apart the city's gas system, releasing fumes that soon caught fire. San Francisco burned for three days. By the time the fires were put out, 500 city blocks had been destroyed. Altogether more than 3,000 people died. Here are reports from some of the survivors.

A ROOM WITH A VIEW

James Hopper, reporter for the *San Francisco Call*, described the scene from his hotel room:

The earth was a rat, shaken in the grinding teeth, shaken, shaken, shaken with periods of slight weariness followed by new bursts of vicious rage. . . .

I got up and walked to the window. I started to open it, but the pane obligingly fell outward and I poked my head out, the floor like a geyser beneath my feet. Then I heard the roar of bricks coming down in cataracts and the groaning of twisted girders all over the city, and at the same time I saw the moon, a calm, pale crescent in the green sky of dawn.

Whose Fault Is That?

San Francisco is located not far from the San Andreas Fault, where the Pacific plate grinds past the North American plate. The fault lies 10 miles (16 km) underground and stretches for 650 miles (1,046 km) along the western edge of California.

CALIFORNIA

● San Francisco

San Andreas Fault

When pressure builds up in the crust surrounding the fault, it is released in shock waves that extend to the surface, shaking the ground and causing earthquakes. The 1906 earthquake measured 7.8 on the Richter scale, the unit of measurement used to determine the magnitude of earthquakes. It was the city's worst earthquake so far, but not the last. . . .

NO VACANCY

Police Lieutenant Henry N. Powell watched a hotel collapse:

As we ran we heard the hotel creak and roar and crash. I turned to look at it. It was then daylight and the dust of the falling buildings had not had time to rise. The hotel lurched forward as if the foundation were dragged backward from under it, and crumpled down over Valencia Street. It did not fall to pieces and spray itself all over the place, but telescoped down on itself like a concertina. This took only a few seconds.

TRAPPED!

William Stehr was stuck under debris in his boarding house in the South of Market area. Eventually, he managed to crawl through the rubble to safety:

Then came another bump, very sudden and very severe. The place fell in on top of me, the breath seemed to be knocked out of my body and I went unconscious.

When my senses came back I was buried and in complete darkness. I tried to feel myself all over, working my limbs as best I could. . . . I guessed that all my bones were intact.

Then I tried to raise myself . . . but the weight of the debris that covered my body was more than I could lift. . . . I heard somebody running over the debris over me, so I shouted for help as loudly as I could.

After that I began to grope and feel about me to find some way of escape. Then I began to hear other agonizing screams for help, and screams of "Fire!"

DANCING BUILDINGS

Police officer Michael Brady was patrolling Market Street:

I ran to the middle of the thoroughfare, and felt like stumbling as I ran because the surface of Market Street was rising and falling like waves on the bay on a stormy day.

I thought I was gone when I saw the Phelan building suddenly lurch over Market Street. But it lurched back again, and as it set back in its place its foundations ripped and cracked and seemed to screech. The tall Call building rocked to and fro from north to south, while the Mutual Bank building on the opposite side of Market Street, near Geary, similarly lurched and dipped over the thoroughfare.

Activity

THE DEADLY WOBBLE Notice how the eyewitnesses often describe the ground moving in waves, like water. New studies suggest that some areas may appear to liquefy during earthquakes. But this doesn't mean that the ground suddenly turns to water—instead, the effects of the shaking ground resemble the movements of liquid when it is disturbed. Mix together a solution of water and potter's clay (available at an art supply store) to see for yourself. Put the solution in a shallow dish, and then blow on it or tap the sides of the dish with a spoon. Observe the results: What shapes form in the dish as the mixture moves? Where do these shapes occur? Use your observations to explain why some areas receive far more damage than others during an earthquake, even though they are right next to each other.

15

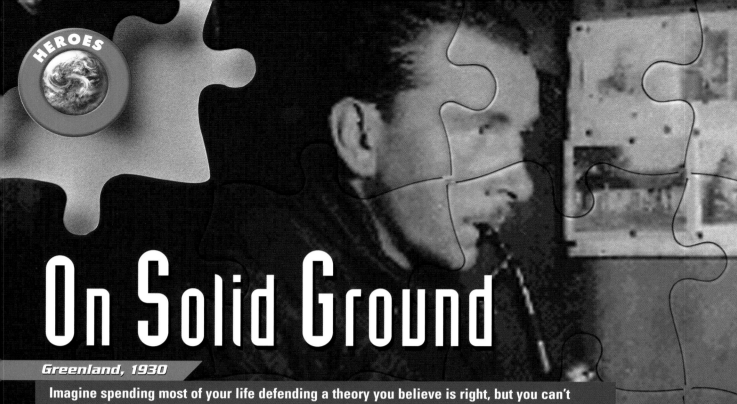

On Solid Ground

Greenland, 1930

Imagine spending most of your life defending a theory you believe is right, but you can't prove it. Others make fun of you and resent your efforts. Even at the end of your life, you know that your great idea is still rejected by most experts in the field.

Welcome to the world of Alfred Wegener.

Today, geologists accept Wegener's theory—called "continental drift"—as fact. He was the first scientist to put forth such a radical idea, and he was ridiculed for it. Even so, he never stopped believing it.

First Steps Toward a New Theory

Trained as an astronomer, Wegener spent most of his life working as a meteorologist. In his work, he became an accomplished explorer, going to Greenland to study the Arctic climate. Wherever he went, he was always making observations and looking for new ways to explain the world around him.

The idea of continental drift first came to Wegener in 1910, after studying the coastlines of the continents on either side of the Atlantic Ocean. Wegener was not the first scientist to observe that the east coast of South America and the west coast of Africa looked like they could fit together, like two pieces of a jigsaw puzzle. But he was the first to explore the evidence that would one day show that they had been one landmass.

Wegener turned to geology and paleontology to prove his theory. One intriguing bit of evidence was the fossil of a small, extinct reptile. The only two places where traces of this creature had been found were Brazil and southern Africa. Wegener argued that this reptile was too small and fragile to be able to swim across the Atlantic, from one continent to the other. After studying certain rocks and plants that were found on both continents but nowhere else in the world, Wegener was convinced: somehow, the continents had once been linked.

But how, since they were now thousands of miles apart? Wegener suggested that *all* of the world's continents had once been joined together in a vast supercontinent, which he named Pangaea [pan-GEE-uh], a word that means "all the earth." This could explain the puzzling fact that fossils of tropical ferns once existed on the island of Spitzbergen, now located in the Arctic. Wegener proposed that about two hundred million years ago, Pangaea began to split apart, and the pieces drifted to other locations on the globe. Wegener briefly set down his theory in 1912, then expanded it three years later in a book titled, *The Origins of Continents and Oceans.*

A Rude Response

Other scientists scorned Wegener's theory. At the time, most geologists believed that land bridges once linked the continents. These bridges explained how the same species of animals could have lived on continents thousands of miles (km) apart. These scientists assumed that Earth's features were fixed: the continents and oceans had always been in the same place. Other critics felt that Wegener had no business publishing theories about geology, since he made his living studying the weather.

The one major flaw with Wegener's theory of continental drift was that he couldn't explain what set the continents in motion. Instead of backing down, though, he continued to gather new evidence, which he used to revise his book. New editions of *The Origins of Continents and Oceans* came out in 1920, 1922, and 1929. Wegener's critics were stubborn as well. As one geologist wrote in 1927, continental drift was a "fantasy . . . that would pop like a soap bubble."

Heroic to the End

While grappling with his new theory, Wegener continued his work in meteorology. In 1930, he helped set up a research station in Greenland, studying the weather patterns through the long Arctic winter. The researchers were stranded at the station by an unexpected blizzard, and Wegener, knowing food supplies were short, volunteered to hike to another station on Greenland's coast. He and his guide both died on the trek. Newspapers praised Wegener as a hero for putting the lives of the others before his own, but it would be some years before scientists began to respect his ground-breaking theory.

Scientists now know that huge plates, several miles (km) thick, lie under Earth's continents and oceans. As heat rises from deep underground, the plates move. This action, known as plate tectonics, explains how the continents have drifted apart in the past and continue to drift today. Wegener had some of the details wrong, but his basic idea was correct—and way ahead of its time.

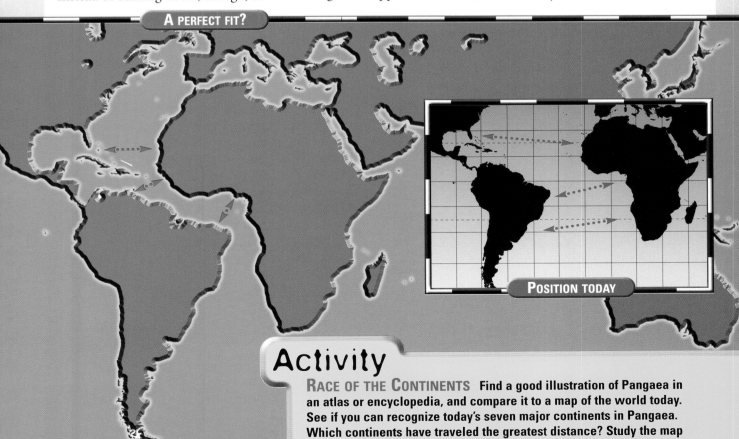

A PERFECT FIT?

POSITION TODAY

Activity

RACE OF THE CONTINENTS Find a good illustration of Pangaea in an atlas or encyclopedia, and compare it to a map of the world today. See if you can recognize today's seven major continents in Pangaea. Which continents have traveled the greatest distance? Study the map on pages 12 and 13: How do the movements of the continents over time relate to the continental plates indicated on the map?

The Many Faces of Mountains

Mountains form in different ways—all of them dramatic. When continents crash into each other, they may "fold" the rocky ground at their edges into mountain ranges. In addition, volcanoes may sprout out of the crust, spewing molten rock, or lava, and getting bigger with each eruption. Mountains and volcanoes also get smaller, as they are eroded over time. And watch out when a volcano decides to blow its top!

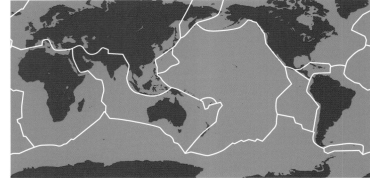

The Indian Subcontinent, 55 Million Years Ago

Make Way for India!

Earth's highest and youngest mountains are the Himalayas, north of India. Once, the subcontinent of India was attached to Africa. Then it broke off and drifted on its own, heading northeast for about 100 million years until it crashed into the Eurasian landmass. India also had to push the oceanic crust out of the way by forcing it under the Eurasian plate. As the Indian plate slid underneath Eurasia, it squeezed layers of the old ocean floor up into jagged folds—the Himalayas.

South America, 150 million years ago

Building the Andes

Under the Pacific Ocean, the Nazca oceanic plate started sliding under the western edge of South America's continental plate. When the plates first collided, part of South America buckled under, creating folds in the crust. This was how the Andes, the longest mountain chain on land (5,500 miles or 8,850 km), were born. The longest mountain range in the world happens to be underwater: the Mid-Ocean Ridge, which stretches for 47,000 miles (75,623 km).

Central Washington, May 18, 1980

Where There's Smoke . . .

Mount St. Helens shot smoke and hot ash 13 miles (21 km) into the atmosphere, leveling forests for miles (km) around. The force of the blast was equal to the explosion of 500 atomic bombs as powerful as the one dropped on Hiroshima at the end of World War II.

Mount St. Helens is part of the "Ring of Fire," a collection of volcanoes that circles the Pacific Ocean. The Ring of Fire follows along the borders of the Pacific plate. As one plate plunges under another, it breaks through to the layer of magma beneath Earth's crust. Pressure inside Earth causes magma to rise; a volcano is basically a "vent" through which magma escapes. Some volcanoes get taller with each eruption, as more layers of magma are added each time. Others, like Mount St. Helens, actually get smaller: in the 1980 eruption, Mount St. Helens lost 1,300 feet (396 m) in elevation.

Mount St. Helens after.

Mount St. Helens before.

Frozen Volcanoes?

Some of the most dramatic land forms are actually the remains of ancient volcanic activity. Devils Tower, an 865-foot (264-m) rock formation in Wyoming, is all that's left of a volcano that was active about 65 million years ago. Once Devils Tower had sloping sides like other mountains, but millions of years of erosion stripped away everything but the stalk of frozen magma, the hardest and most durable part of the ancient volcano. According to an Indian legend, Devils Tower rose out of the ground to save a girl who was being chased by a bear. The ruts on the side of the rock were formed by the bear's claws as he tried (and failed) to climb up to the top. More recently, Devils Tower had a starring role in the science fiction movie *Close Encounters of the Third Kind*.

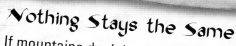

Nothing Stays the Same

If mountains don't last forever, then what does?

Alfred Lord Tennyson wonders just that in this excerpt from his poem, "In Memoriam."

The hills are shadows, and they flow
From form to form, and nothing stands;
They melt like mist, the solid lands,
Like clouds they shape themselves and go.

MOUNTAIN MYTHS

People in ancient times didn't know about plate tectonics, so they shared stories with each other to explain how mountains formed.

Holy Battle: According to a Klamath Indian legend, the Cascade Range of the Pacific Northwest was the result of a war between gods of the Below World and gods of the After World.

Lying Around: A Tibetan myth says that the Himalayas were formed when an evil princess stretched out on the ground and died.

Boning Up: The Vikings believed that a race of frost giants, led by Ymir, created the universe. Ymir was later defeated and killed by his descendants, who used his body to create heaven and Earth. Ymir's bones became the mountains. His hair became the trees, his teeth were turned into rocks, and the clouds formed out of his brain.

EGG-streme Beginnings: Pan-gu was a Chinese giant who came out of a cosmic egg. He grew for thousands of years until he burst apart. Pieces of his head became China's sacred mountains.

North America, 300 Million Years Ago

From Mountain to Molehill

Mountains also shrink over time. Today, the highest peak in the Appalachians is about 6,700 feet (2,042 m) high, and most of the range is much lower. But about 300 million years ago, when the Appalachians first formed, they were perhaps as high as the Rockies, which have many peaks above 10,000 feet (3,048 m). Over time, rivers and glaciers wore the Appalachians down. Unlike the steep, craggy summits of much "younger" mountain ranges such as the Alps or the Himalayas, the Appalachians have soft, rounded peaks. This is your first clue that the Appalachians are much older.

Baby, It's

A North American glacier.

It's Long

Before it gets too freezing in here, let's go back up. Your bobsled breaks through to fresh air, and once again you're on the surface. From here, the glacier looks like a snow-covered mountain slope, stretching out as far as you can see downhill. Let's see what this bobsled can do—hold on!

Along the way, you ride over smooth parts. You're not going too fast because it's not very steep. It is a giant field of snow and ice, covering every inch

Get out of the way! You're in a mountain valley, looking at a wall of ice, snow, and rocks. It may be flowing slowly—the fastest go only about six feet (2 m) per day—but a glacier stops for nobody. Anything in its path—rocks, dirt, hills—gets pushed aside or swallowed up in the ice.

It's Deep

You've got a special enclosed glacier bobsled, equipped with a set of rotating blades that lets you drill through the ice. But before you go zooming off downhill to the end of the glacier, let's take a look inside. This glacier is deep—probably several hundred feet (m) at least. It sits in a bowl-shaped hollow between several mountain peaks. Crank the blades!

The top layer is a cinch, just layers of freshly fallen snow. But below that, your bobsled has to drill its way through compressed snow and then layer after layer of ice. Because it's so cold in the mountains, snow keeps falling but doesn't get a chance to melt. It just gets covered by new layers of snow, which then get compressed into ice. Just how deep IS this thing? The ice just keeps going and going. Don't expect this to be like jumping into the deep end of a swimming pool. Instead, think of a twenty-story building, and you're in the elevator, going down.

Cold in Here!

of the valley floor. Suddenly, you get to a steep part. The glacier is now nothing but massive ice blocks with huge cracks between them. These are called crevasses, and you don't want to fall down into them. Some might be 50 feet (15 m) deep or more.

Back to smooth sledding. The slope is less steep now, and it's nice to be grooving along the ice. Sure looks dirty, though; it doesn't snow as much at this lower altitude, so what you're seeing are chunks of dirt and rocks embedded in the old ice. The glacier picks rocks up on its way downhill, or wind blows dirt from the surrounding hillsides.

Now you're at the end. It's slushy here—the ice is definitely melting more down here than back at the top. Everywhere you can hear the sound of running water. The ground is soggy. This mighty river of ice comes to an end in nothing but a pile of rocks and dirt (called a terminal moraine) and a muddy pond.

It Stops for Nothing

A glacier is relentless. Its enormous weight will change the landscape completely. How do you know? Well, step aside! It turns out your bobsled can speed up time. This means you can stand back and watch the whole glacier pass you by. What would normally take several hundred years happens before your eyes in a matter of minutes. Let's see what this glacier can do.

You hear ice and rock scraping against rock. You see mounds of earth pushed aside. The whole mass moves as fast as an avalanche or a mudflow. And then it's gone! As if it had never been here in the first place.

But it has! Everywhere you look, the landscape says GLACIER WAS HERE. Check out that big boulder. Its color and texture don't look anything like the rocks nearby; most likely the glacier carried it here from far away. You glance down at the rock under your feet. Note the scratches on the surface, all going in the same direction. Something big and heavy was using dirt and pebbles like a scouring pad against the rock—what else could it be but the glacier?

Even the U shape of the valley bears glacier traces. It's as if someone took a giant ice cream scoop to the land. Back at the top, you see how the glacier has carved out a circular shape between the mountain peaks. All that's left of the glacier is a small alpine lake, made from the melted snow and ice. Who would've thought that just gently falling snow would make such a difference in the shape of the land?

Activity

LANDSCAPE SCULPTURE Huge glaciers covered about 30 percent of all land on Earth about 18,000 years ago. This was an era known as the Great Ice Age. At its peak, ice covered much of the Northern Hemisphere, including much of North America, Europe, and Russia. Then the average climate got warmer, and many of the glaciers melted away. It was only one of many ice ages in Earth's history.

If you live in the northern United States, go to a local state park and look around. Write down as many features that might have been caused by glaciers as you can find. Study the shape of valleys and hills as well as the surfaces of rock outcroppings. What does the evidence tell you about which direction the glaciers moved?

If you don't live in an area affected by the last Ice Age, go to your library and look at landscape photography books of places that were, such as the Alps, the Rocky Mountains, the Norwegian coast, Scotland, Wales, and others. Look for pictures of features caused by glaciers. Make a list of what you find, identifying the examples by location and glacier effect. Write your own caption for each one, in which you describe what the glacier did to create that formation.

Earth: Inside and Out

The Core of the Matter Earth is bubbling with activity. Let's take a look.

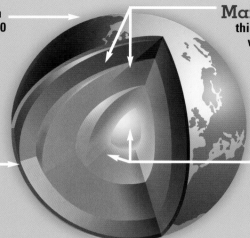

Atmosphere: Collection of gases that extends about 1,000 miles (1,609 km) into space. Close to the surface, nitrogen makes up 78 percent of the atmosphere; most of the rest is oxygen.

Crust: Earth's solid surface. Under the oceans, the crust is mostly basalt, about 3 to 7 miles (5 to 11 km) thick. Under the continents it's thicker—up to 40 miles (64 km).

Mantle: At about 1,800 miles (2,896 km) thick, this makes up 85 percent of Earth's volume. The top part is sometimes called "plastic" because although it's solid, it moves. The outer part of the mantle and the crust together are called the *lithosphere*. The *lithosphere* consists of huge plates that move continually.

Core: Earth's center. The *outer core*, about 1,400 miles (2,253 km) thick, is mostly liquid iron, along with nickel and other elements. The *inner core*, about 800 miles (1,287 km) thick, is solid and 9,000°F (4,982°C).

Super Sleuthing Years and years of observing rock samples, fossils, and other evidence, combined with a lot of deep and creative thought, have helped scientists uncover some secrets of Earth's structure and history. And one key discovery often led to another down the line. Here are some highlights of their work.

Rocks as Evidence: In the 1780s, James Hutton develops idea that current rocks hold clues to Earth's past by observing rocks in his native Scotland. Hutton also suggests Earth is much older than previously thought.

Earth's Age →

Radiometric Dating: In 1907, Bertram Boltwood provides method for dating rocks using radioactivity; Boltwood puts Earth's age at 2.2 billion years.

Earth's Age →

Meteorite Analysis: In 1953, Clair Patterson puts Earth's age at 4.6 billion years after studying lead in meteorites and rock samples.

Clues from Space →

Iridium Found in Ancient Rocks: In 1980, Luis and Walter Alvarez discover samples of iridium, which is rare on Earth and may have been carried here on meteorites that collided with Earth about 65 million years ago; leads to theory that meteorite collision may have wiped out dinosaurs.

Earth's Crust →

Theory of Continental Drift: In 1912, Alfred Wegener proposes idea of supercontinent Pangaea that broke apart; says continents are still drifting.

Ocean Floor →

Mid-Ocean Ridge: In 1958, Bruce Heezen and Marie Tharp discover vast mountain range at the ocean floor, extending around the globe for 47,000 miles (75,623 km).

Ocean Floor →

Seafloor Spreading: In 1960, Harry Hess develops the notion that seafloor spreads from giant rifts at bottom of the oceans; proof of this leads to idea of plate tectonics and confirms Wegener's theory of continental drift.

Below the Surface →

Origin of Earthquakes: In 1927, Kiyoo Wadati shows that some earthquakes begin deep in Earth's crust, although they are felt on the surface.

Below the Surface →

Earth's Inner and Outer Core: In 1936, after studying seismic waves caused by earthquakes, Inge Lehmann proposes that Earth's center is solid rather than molten liquid and that it is composed of an outer and an inner core.

Get Your Spheres Here

Scientists classify everything in, on, and above Earth into four main categories, or spheres. You've already read about the atmosphere. Here are the others.

Atmosphere — The collection of gases that surround Earth.

Biosphere — All living things on the planet.

Lithosphere — Earth's crust and mantle.

Hydrosphere — Water in all its forms: solid, liquid, and gaseous.

Plates with a Past

Think today's continents always sat where they do now? No way—these landmasses are long-time movers and shakers.

800–700 Million Years Ago
All continents came together to form Rodinia.

600 Million Years Ago
Continent of Gondwana begins to form. Includes: Australia, Antarctica, South America, Africa, and India.

450 Millions Years Ago
Lapetus Ocean separates the continents of Laurentia and Baltica, which form part of Europe and North America.

250 Million Years Ago
"Supercontinent" Pangaea, surrounded by one "superocean" called Panthalassa.

200–130 Million Years Ago
Gondwana splits off from Pangaea; formation of oceans as continents drift apart: Atlantic, Indian, and Pacific Oceans.

Clues from Space

Meteorite Crater Found off Mexico: In 1987, Charles Duller finds first surface evidence of a meteorite impact possibly related to extinction of the dinosaurs.

Clues from Space

Discovery of Meteorite Fragment: In 1995, while examining samples from the Pacific Ocean floor, Frank Kyte finds what may be evidence of the meteorite that may have wiped out dinosaurs.

Ocean Floor

Ocean Vents Exploration: In 1977, Robert Ballard and others unexpectedly find sea creatures near vents deep at ocean floor; may have been source of all life on Earth.

Ocean Floor

Activity

HOW MUCH IS A MILLION? Earth's history is measured in millions of years. To understand "million," get a group of your friends and discuss collecting a million toothpicks, pennies, bottle caps, or small rocks. Since we use a base 10 number system, organize your collection as follows: 10 groups of 10 into sandwich baggies; 10 groups of 100 into larger-sized freezer baggies; 10 groups of 1000 into a grocery bag. How many of each bag will you need for the entire collection?

AMAZING BUT TRUE

Get a Life!

I n its early days, Earth was a rocky wasteland of volcanoes and meteor craters. No separate continents, no oceans, no oxygen. Today, it is home to all kinds of living creatures—including you. As far as we know, Earth is the only planet in the Solar System that can support life. But how did this happen? And when exactly did life begin on Earth? Biologists, chemists, physicists, astronomers, geologists, and even mathematicians all ponder this question. They look at rocks and fossils to figure out how life evolved through time. They study the different forms of life and their environments. They also make calculations and do experiments; some scientists have actually tried to create life in the laboratory.

Readin' the Rocks

Fossils are the bones, cells, tracks, imprints (molds), and chemical remains of things that were once alive. The fossil record tells us that not all life began on Earth at the same time. Bacteria formed before plants; fish arrived before mammals. Crocodiles have been on Earth for about 250 million years. Humans have been around for less than 1 million years. And some creatures, such as trilobites, lived for millions of years and then died out.

Did you know that some rocks are actually made of the remains of living things? Starting about 550 million years ago, the skeletons and shells of tiny marine creatures began to pile up on the seafloor. This layer eventually hardened into limestone. Lush, swampy forests grew on land 350 million years ago. When the plants died, they were buried in mud and eventually became layers of coal. That's why coal is considered a "fossil fuel."

Life in the Deepest Depths

On the bottom of the ocean, 1.5 miles (2.4 km) below the surface, lava oozes out of volcanic ridges. Nearby vents spew water as hot as 400° C (750° F) out into the near-freezing ocean water. Believe it or not, this is home for quite a few forms of life, including spider crabs, clams, snails, blind shrimp, tubeworms, and bacteria. Because sunlight, an energy source for most forms of life, doesn't penetrate this far down, these creatures somehow live off the chemicals in the hot springs.

Scientists have also found life forms in extremely salty bodies of water (such as the Dead Sea and Great Salt Lake), in pools of frozen methane-water in the Gulf of Mexico, and deep within rocks in Oregon. Some of these creatures are very primitive one-celled organisms collectively known as archaea (from a Greek word meaning "ancient" or "primitive"). The discovery of archaea got scientists to reconsider everything they'd thought about the origins of life. Maybe, for example, sunlight isn't necessary for life to begin. Maybe even oxygen isn't necessary!

Back to the Basics

All living things are made of chemical compounds. But where did these compounds come from in the first place? Could they have formed in space and gotten here from comets and meteorites, which collided with Earth long ago? Or did lightning strikes, meteorite impacts, or ultraviolet sunlight force atoms to react with each other to form the compounds on Earth? Scientists known as astrobiologists examine the composition of comets, meteorites, and inter-stellar dust to find out more.

How to Get There

Before you can study the hydrothermal vents at the bottom of the ocean, you have to get down there. Researchers squeeze into tiny submersible vessels, which are launched from ships, and "dive" down thousands of feet (m) to the ocean floor. And someone has to be at the controls, both to pilot the submersible and collect the samples for study.

Meet Cindy Lee Van Dover, Ph.D. She is a biologist and also a former pilot of the research submersible *Alvin*, used by the Woods Hole Oceanographic Institute. Before each launch, she's got to make sure everything's working properly, going through a thirteen-page checklist of safety and operating procedures with other technicians before each launch. Once the dive is underway, she has to monitor *Alvin's* equipment constantly and communicate with the research ship. On a typical mission, *Alvin* can descend more than 7,000 feet (2,134 m). It gets dark quickly—after 1,000 feet (305 m) there is hardly any sunlight visible. Once *Alvin* reaches the ocean floor, a strobe light helps Cindy navigate. She operates at a speed of no more than 2 miles (3 km) an hour, so researchers can find what they are looking for. Robotic arms collect specimens and samples for further study. "The return ascent was the most relaxing part of the day," Cindy says, recalling one particular assignment. Back on deck of the research ship, "another long list of post-dive checks awaited, followed by any repairs that needed to be made to the sub. These were long days at sea, from 5:30 A.M. to 7, 8, 9, 10 or later at night, depending on what needed to be fixed."

Activity

SETTING THE SCENE What do you think Earth was like when life first formed? Read more about it and then draw a landscape of Earth 3.5 billion years ago. Don't forget the Moon and the meteorites and comets that were flying near Earth's orbit. Remember that there were no tree, birds, clouds, or even blue sky.

"What's That Doing Here?"

Phakding, Nepal, 2000

Geologist Dr. Janet Lzuhu is back in her hometown, checking out the latest find. It's her job to look into any evidence relating to the formation of the Himalayas, and this time, some very interesting objects have turned up practically in her family's own backyard.

Her niece and nephew, Shana and Lhotse, were playing in the fields outside of town and came upon the items on the riverbank. One is a fossil of a sea creature, one is a lump of coal, and the third is a piece of igneous rock. Shana and Lhotse have already showed the samples to a group of scientists passing through on a geological expedition. They sent the children away, telling them that someone must have planted the items by the river, just to confuse dedicated scientists such as themselves.

This isn't the first time Dr. Lzuhu has been asked to answer some questions about strange rocks. As ever growing numbers of hikers come through the area aiming for the top of Mount Everest, it seems that more and more mysterious items are being found in the ground near the village. One year it was an Indian arrowhead—American Indian—which turned out to be some hiker's good luck charm.

It's no wonder that so many people are passing through this village 9,000 feet (2,743 m) above sea level. The village is only several miles from Mount Everest, the point at which Earth's crust is at its thickest. Growing up in the shadow of these jagged peaks of limestone and other rock, Dr. Lzuhu always knew she would dedicate her life to the study of mountains. And in her mind, there are no more magnificent mountains than the Himalayas, formed over forty million years ago when India drifted north and crashed into Asia. Two continents, two sets of sedimentary layers formed over billions of years, and one dramatic uplift made these mountains what they are. Dr. Lzuhu has since learned that the Himalayas are still getting taller.

Dr. Lzuhu takes a close look at the three objects. In her work, she's seen many other rocks just like these. The fossil is a certain kind of cephalopod. This one is an extinct sea animal with a coiled shell, which she estimates to be about 135 million years old. The coal is anthracite, a type of coal that is usually found deep in the earth. The igneous rock was formed from volcanic ash that hardened after cooling.

She turns to Shana and Lhotse and asks them if they found anything else at all similar to these rocks where they were playing.

"We looked all around, thinking we would," Lhotse replies. "But nothing else turned up. That's why we think the scientists might be right."

"The scientists are only partly right," Dr. Lzuhu says. "Two of these things were definitely brought here by someone else. But it's very possible—in fact it's likely—that one of these three things actually did come from around here. It could have been buried in the ground and then uncovered by the water running through the stream. Come with me. We'll explain to them why we think they might be wrong." The three of them head off to the camp where the scientists are busily collecting rock samples.

What does Dr. Lzuhu say to the scientists? Which of the two objects does she rule out and why? Explain why the third item could have been found in the Himalayan region. Can you describe where it might have come from and the natural forces that moved it to where the children found it?

PAKISTAN

NEPAL

INDIA

Bay of Bengal

SRI LANKA

Use these clues . . . **Clues**

- Anthracite is the compressed remains of plants and trees from vast swamps that dominated land on Earth more than 300 million years ago.

- Coal is found in large deposits, deep under the surface of Earth.

- Volcanoes can occur where an oceanic plate slides under a continental plate and into the molten rock under the crust.

Answer on page 32.

POOR EARTH! It's really taken a beating over the past 4.5 billion years. It's been bombarded by meteorites and comets from outer space; it's been rocked by earthquakes; it's been carved and eroded away by glaciers and running water. Even the wind won't give Earth a rest. But all this weathering sure shapes Earth into some beautiful works of art.

A River Runs through It

Give running water enough time, and it will carve its own way through solid rock. Some rocks are softer than others, allowing the river to shape the land in truly awe-inspiring ways. Rivers scoop out dirt and rock from one place and deposit them in another. This means they rarely run straight; more often you'll see meandering canyons where the river has created its own winding course.

SUPER BOWL

What happens when a rock more than 100 feet (30 m) across falls out of the sky? It makes a hole in the ground, that's what. Meteor Crater near Winslow, Arizona, was created when a meteorite struck Earth about 25,000 years ago. It's about 4,100 feet (1,250 m) across and 600 feet (183 m) deep. Earth has been bombarded by meteorites and comets since day one, but there aren't many craters left to tell the tale. Why? Because weather, erosion, and plate tectonics are constantly changing the surface of the planet and wiping all traces of craters away.

SAND AND STONE

Water's Only the Beginning...

As it strips away layers of rock and carries pebbles downstream, water also exposes other layers of rock to erosion by wind and rain. What you get is spectacular landscape like Bryce Canyon, Utah. Water and weather worked together over millions of years to make these strange landforms, called hoodoos, which the Paiute Indians believed were once a magical race of people turned to stone by the Coyote Spirit.

GETTING DOWN TO THE HARD STUFF

Sometimes, erosion uncovers rock that never before saw the light of day. Deep underground, molten rock, or magma, slowly cooled into large reservoirs of granite. These chunks of granite are exposed when the rock layers above are slowly scraped away by water, weather, and glaciers. The Half Dome in Yosemite, California, was once buried deep underground, believe it or not.

The Sands of Time

Wind erodes by blowing off small pieces of rock. It is particularly effective in desert areas, where there aren't any trees to protect Earth from wind's relentless force. Wind also kicks up sand and pebbles from the ground; these can dig out the base of a rock pedestal and sculpt it into a mushroom or wine-glass shape.

Activity

MAKE YOUR OWN MESA Harder rock can protect the layers underneath it from erosion. The land around it might wear away from rain and wind, but the rock will remain, as a flat-topped formation called a *mesa* (meaning "table" in Spanish). Fill a shallow plate with sand and then place a few pennies in the sand. Simulate rain by using a watering can to sprinkle water over the sand (or position the plate near a lawn sprinkler or a spray hose in the kitchen sink). Observe what happens to the sand underneath the pennies. Describe what happened. Can you explain how this demonstration is similar to the formation of a mesa?

29

A Garden of Earthly Delights

Earthy Humor

Why didn't Earth swallow the land?

Because it didn't like the crusts.

Why did the continent feel overworked?

Because it had too much on its plate.

What do San Franciscans eat for breakfast?

Quaker Oats.

Where on Earth do you find green icebergs?

Look in your supermarket's produce section!

Earth Facts 'n Figures

● It would take you 304 days to dig through Earth, if you could progress at a rate of 1 mile per hour (1.6 kph)—and if you could stand the heat.

● It would take you 17 days to travel around the globe, at the equator, if you were travelling at a speed of 60 miles per hour (96.5 kph).

● It would take you, traveling at 60 miles (96.5 km) per hour, 13 days to circle the globe if you were at the tropic of Cancer or Capricorn.

Big and Still Growing

The highest place on Earth is the top of Mount Everest, in the Himalayas. For years, the official elevation was 29,028 feet (8,848 m). But in May 1999, a team of climbers with state-of-the-art instruments discovered that Everest is actually two meters higher: 29,035 feet (8,850 m), to be exact. Did Everest actually grow taller since the last elevation measurement? Yes and no. Techniques and devices for measuring altitude are much more precise nowadays, so the earlier figure wasn't quite accurate. But Everest is getting taller every year, as the Indian continent continues to push underneath Asia, driving the whole mountain range higher in the sky.

Layers upon Layers

There are nine major kinds of rocks in the Grand Canyon. The upper ones are the youngest, but they all have weird names. Here's a good way to remember them, the next time you take a hike from the rim down to the bottom:

Know	**K**aibab Limestone	250 million years old
The	**T**oroweap Formation	255 million years old
Canyon's	**C**oconino Sandstone	260 million years old
History,	**H**ermit Shale	265 million years old
Study	**S**upai Formation	285 million years old
Rocks	**R**edwall Limestone	335 million years old
Made	**M**uav Limestone	515 million years old
By	**B**right Angel Shale	530 million years old
Time	**T**apeats Sandstone	545 million years old

Oh, and there's one more, the real old-timer:

Vishnu Schist	825–1,700 million years old

Fanciful Fossils

People had all sorts of explanations for fossils before they understood that these rocks were the remains of ancient organisms. One theory in the 1400s said that fossils came from small seeds made of stone. These stone creatures lived and died deep inside Earth.

Planet Slang

We may not always appreciate the firm, solid earth under our feet, but we refer to it all the time in everyday speech. Here are some common Earth-related expressions:

Groundbreaking: new and different

Earth-shattering: so new and different it's revolutionary

Down to earth: no-nonsense; unpretentious

Down and dirty: no frills; basic

Global: all encompassing; overall

Splittin' Up

You know by now that Europe and North America were once one piece of land. (This was long before America was one of England's colonies, by the way.) But did you know that they are still separating? Lasers from two separate locations on the globe can calculate the continents' exact position by bouncing off mirrors on satellites. They have determined that Europe and North America are moving apart from each other at a speed of .8 inches (2 cm) per year.

Over its history, Earth has had at least four major ice ages, during which the planet's average temperature cooled significantly. Lower temperatures caused the polar ice caps to become thicker and broader, spreading over portions of the continents and locking up much of the planet's water supply in ice. Some say we are now in a warming period and that the ice caps will melt before temperatures cool again.

But what if the opposite were true? What if we were in a cooling period and about to enter another ice age? Soon you and your friends will be in charge of the world. What would you do if the ice sheets in Antarctica and Greenland were due to increase dramatically in the next five years? Currently, 29 percent of the earth is land, and 71 percent is water. Only 10 percent of the water is ice. This figure could increase to as much as 25 percent.

Some changes can be predicted immediately: the sea level will fall, creating more land area but reducing the water supply. Temperatures will be much colder and for longer periods of time. Glaciers will form and spread once again. But what do these changes mean for life on the planet? How will human life be affected? Based on what you now know about the history of Earth, what can be done to minimize the impact of this enormous shift in global climate?

Gather friends and teammates around and:

1. Estimate how much more land could be uncovered as sea levels drop. Where would it be located? Study topographical maps of the ocean floor and other resources to make educated guesses.

2. Discuss the implications of this "new land." Who would it belong to? Will political boundaries between nations be affected? What are some ways to prepare for potential problems in this area?

3. Some forms of life may not survive. Should you take steps to preserve species that might otherwise face extinction, or should you let natural forces take their course (as they have done in the past)? Weigh the pros and cons.

4. Study Earth's climate and calculate what it might be like during an ice age. What parts of the globe will be the warmest? What parts might become too cold to be hospitable to human life?

5. A large percentage of the human population lives in urban areas, some of which might be threatened by the approach of glaciers. Using the most recent ice age as a model, draw a scenario for the major cities of North America. Devise a relocation plan for the cities in the greatest danger.

6. After collecting all this information and discussing it with your colleagues, draw up a detailed scenario of what you expect will happen during this ice age. Produce one report for each area: biosphere, hydrosphere, lithosphere, and atmosphere. Then write up your recommendations for preparations and survival.

ANSWERS Solve-It-Yourself Mystery, pages 26–27

The correct item was the fossil. The coal and igneous rock were planted by someone else. Anthracite is buried in large deposits deep underground, yet this sample was found as just one lump. The children saw nothing else like it nearby. This fact is also a giveaway for the igneous rock, which was formed from hardened volcanic ash. Where there's one sample of igneous rock of this type, there should be many. When volcanoes release hot ash or lava, they release a lot of it.

Also, there are no active volcanoes in the Himalayas. These mountains are at the thickest point of Earth's crust, where two continents are colliding. Volcanoes are links between the surface and the molten rock under Earth's crust. They occur where ocean plates are being forced under continental plates, not where two continental plates are directly abutting and pushing each other up—the molten rock is simply too far down to seek a way out through a volcano.

The Himalayas were formed of sedimentary rocks. One of these is limestone, which began as sediment under the ocean, made of plant and animal matter. So finding a fossil in limestone is not unusual. Limestone is part of the Himalayas because there was once an ocean between India and Asia. When India collided with Asia, it pushed the ocean crust out of the way. This ocean crust was then thrust upward, forming part of the Himalayas.

J 550 Gar

Earth's History
    (Our Planet Earth)

DATE DUE			
JUN 0 6 2008